JUST BECAUSE OF ME

JUST BECAUSE OF ME

Oh! My love
Just because of me
You became a laughing stock
Just because of me
You became poor for me to be rich
Just because of me
You came down from heaven
And took the flesh of man
Just because of me
You became a slave
Just because of me
You accepted to die on the cross
Just because of me
You humbled yourself
All these you've done for me
I owe you obedience totally
Because you did not count equality with God
A thing to be grasped
All these Jesus did
For all of humankind.

JUST BECAUSE OF YOU

Oh! My love
Just because of you
I took the risk of my life
Just because of you
I left my people to go to an unknown place
Just because of you
I accepted to live with a people I know not
Just because of you
I forfeited all the pleasures of my life
Just because of you
I agreed to pass through the torrents of the water
Just because of you
I entered the rivers and stayed for hours
Just because of you
I saw my mission in Africa as your will
Just because of you
I've accepted all the difficulties on my way
Just because of you
I've sacrificed all that I have
Some had done it before
The early Christians did it
Going through trials
Just because of you
They left the enjoyment of their fatherland
Towards far distant isles they went
Showing the light to the nations that encountered them.
(continued…)

Today like the apostles
I am in Africa
A continent of natural beauty
Like the early Fathers of the Church
Who sacrificed all they had
Just because of you
I have come to do the same
You never deserted them
Never desert me, O my love, my God
For I am here
To do your will
Just because of you.

*(IN HONOUR OF THE EARLY CHRISTIAN
MISSIONARIES)*

EMBRACE LOVE AND GET HEALING

Oh! Poor me
I have committed the greatest crime
The worst vice
Rejecting love
A gift was freely given to me
By my savior
How painful it is
To refuse a gift freely given
My love for sin has caused this
For out of love he died for me
Taking my place of death
Unrepentant I have become
Despite all his pleas for me
I have kept deaf ears to his calling
I have sought him day and night
But have not found him
I am despondent, bewildered
This failure has hurt my being
I have groaned in travail
Like a woman in labor
But he has not listened to me
Because my sin has blocked the way
But when I recovered myself
His light like a cloud hangs over me
He heard my cry and God said
"It's over
For every problem has a solution
The solution to yours is
Sin no more against love
Embrace love and get healing."

I WILL GIVE YOU MY LIFE

I wonder why you love me
I've often pondered why
I'm not the most articulate
I'm not the most handsome
Nor am I the richest
Yet, of all things that are
You gave me your love
Why can't I give you mine?
If not for anything
I will give it for the sake of love
The most significant gift of life is love
For in life there is love
For without love there'll be no life
Love urges us to live in sacrifice
Love calls us to move on amidst trials
Love pushes us to hope more than despair
Love urges us to be faithful at all times
Amidst trials and death
Love sustains us
You gave me your love
You've given me your life
I will pay back with love
For without this love of yours
There'll be no love of mine
Of all the things I have in life
None of them can repay you
For in you there's real love
Since you've loved me so
I owe you, my love
I will give you my life.

LOVE: A THING OF THE WILL

Have you ever encountered love?
Where did you find it?
How did you feel?
O! Splendid!
For love is a thing of the will
The will says, 'love'
The body says, 'yes.'
Without the will
The body cannot love
For the will desires
And the body affirms in action
O! How lovely it is
To discover that
Love is a thing of the will
The will to say yes
And the will to say no
Once the will says yes
Love unfolds its true fragrance
The sweet and odoriferous smell
To love without boundaries
Is a thing of the will.

THE WONDER OF LOVE

Oh, how mysterious you are
O great love
Your mystery surpasses all
For you are our foundation
Though immaterial
More material yet, than the material things
Unseen yet does more
Than physical work
O! Great love
Many seek you
In fighting hatred and greed
And all other vices
But your mystery they've lost
Forever in search they are
But thy light eluded them
Where are you?
O ruler and mover of the universe
Teach the world to know
That there is no greater
Mystery in this world than
The wonder of love.

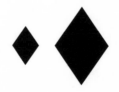

I WILL BE WITH YOU FOREVER

Where were you?
I sought you
But couldn't find you
I sought you in my heart
You were not there
In my books, I sought for you
Yet, you were not there
In the silence of my heart
Your voice like a thousand bells
Rang like a thunderstorm
Here am I since you want me
How joyful my heart was
Since I have found my love
The joy of my heart
Whom for a million times
I have sought
Yet, in the depth of my heart
Lies you like a forgotten edifice
At the outskirts of a city
I am yours since I found you
You are mine since you chose me
I have sought you
But you have found me
I will be with you forever.

EVERYWHERE LOVE

Everywhere people speak about love
In fact, love is the only language
Both living and non-living understand
Show love to a fellow human being
All in turn, will become happier
Show love to a plant
It grows well
Show love to an environment
It becomes a pleasant environment
Show love to a house
It becomes a home
What can love not do?
God is love
Since God is love
And love is God
God is everywhere
So everywhere love

SCALE OF LOVE

Love has many scales
With which it is measured
But the greatest scale
With which it is measured
Can't be found anywhere
Neither can it be bought elsewhere
It is not far-fetched
It is not in a foreign land
The best scale that can measure love
Is the full extent of self
Christ gave himself
Not in words but in deeds
What can you do for others?
Use the best scale of love
That is yourself
What will be good for you
Will be good for another
Love your neighbor as yourself
That is the scale of love.

LOVE IS THE SAME EVERY TIME

Every time we go around doing good
By loving and caring for everyone
We are spreading the aroma of love
This means that:
Everything we do for the sake of love
Even if we are not appreciated with love
Will never go in vain for the sake of love
If only we keep listening to the voice of love
We will be able to endure for the sake of love
Since anyone who is nurtured in love
Will always trust in love
Despite the shortcomings from others
They who love live for others
Even if they are not loved by others
They still love every time
Because love lives in them every time
They will never waver any time
Even life is not the same every time
Love is the same every time
Even though time may change
Love is the same every time and will never change
This is why from age to age
Even when we turn every page
Love is the same every time.

THE BATTLE FIELD OF LOVE AND LUST

In the battlefield of human relationship
Look at the reasons why you should love
If you don't verify every love, you might be dealing with
lust
If don't accept true love you have given room for lust
because "nature abhors vacuum."
If you don't listen to the voice of love, you may miss the
message that would have saved you eternal regrets. This
can be done by allowing emotions which emanate from
lust to overrule you.
If you don't endure in trials that come from love, you
might lose the only love that you would have gotten in this
world.
If you are not so fast in understanding the intricacies of
love, you might be taken on a ride like a fool by lust.
If you don't trust in love, there can never be genuine love
in your relationship. Just give a forum for failure yet trust,
for no one is perfect.
If you don't integrate this love, you cannot have an
introspective change which is the best change, for without
it there can never be an expressive love.
If you don't nurture love like you nurture a human being, it
will wither like flowers in the desert.
If you don't express your feelings of love to the people you
love, you may die at last without getting that love.
Love is like a magnetic appliance that attracts, just like
how the nectar attracts the bee. Open wide your nectar,
that is your willingness; then you will draw your love
away from lust.

WHEN I HATE YOU

When I hate you
I have said no to happiness
When I hate you
I have shut the door from above
When I hate you
I have turned away from light
When I hate you
I have expelled myself from life
This is why it is more harmful to me
Than the one I hate
Since I live with the pain
That'll hurt me greatly
Even if I am thousands of miles away
And the distant like from the end of the sea to the coast
The pain will be as wide as the sea
I will put myself through suffering
Because of what will benefit me nothing
Something that will sap all my energy
And snuff life out of me
Because I think I gain by hating you
Oh what a poor decision I have made
I have not been the same
O God, help me not to hate anyone
Even when they have hurt me
Because you never hate anyone
You are always patient with us
Even when we err every now and then
May we always remember that when we hate
We have been led astray
Into perpetual chains of unhappiness.

FOR THE SAKE OF LOVE

For the sake of love
We need to stand at each other's side
This is why we need to sacrifice
In order to be together
We have been created to live in a community
Which we can build together
For the sake of love
That is the basis of our foundation

Because unless we do things for the sake of love
We may not be able to anything without insincerity
Even when we are in friendships
We'll always remember that everyone has a problem
Since no one is perfect
We will always endure for the sake of love
We can always stand with one another
For the sake of love
Then think of the harm
We'll cause our lives
If we walk out on each other
When we would have given each other hope
That no matter how hard life may be
We will always succeed
This is why we should not stop loving each other
Even when things are not moving well
Because if we're the center of each other's life
No pain will push us away from each other
This is because everything will be easy
For the sake of love

LOVE

Man cannot do without love
The world cannot be without love
There would be no life without love
There would be no peace without love
Without love, nothing moves
One cannot love without sacrifice
For love without sacrifice is abuse
Sacrifice without love is fruitless
To think of love is to think of life
You cannot love a person
Without knowing the inner person
To encounter love,
Is to encounter change
Love makes a man see from another perspective
To love is to begin to be
For if you are not loving
You are not living
Think of love
And have peace of mind
Which can only be gotten
From the seed of love.

TWO PHRASES THAT MOVE ME

There're two phrases that move me
They also move you
I mean you
They can change you
What do these do to you:
I love you and
I need you
These two phrases show how we are valued
Whenever we hear them
We believe them
Even when they are not meant
Because they are sweet things
That can change the life of the lonely
They give joy to the sorrowful

LOVE IS ACTION

Love can best be proved in action
Not in words
For action speaks louder than words
Above these there is
Nothing that I see
In you, I have found
The meaning of love
Which for ages I have sought
Going through seas and oceans
You are the ship that carries me
In this journey of love
In turbulence and crisis of the sea
I will go down with the ship
If it is sinking
That is to say
I will never leave you
For anything at all
Because love is action
You have shown me, love
You gave me life
Even when I deserve death
You gave me hope
When I was in despair
You gave me joy
When I was in sorrow
I will die in you O Lord

WHAT LOVE DOES TO HUMANS

Love does many things to us
The force of love brings us out
It makes us see the importance
Of others around us
It makes us see the needs of others
At most it takes us to a place that teaches us
That without love
There is no joy in this life
Hence love is the controlling power
Of the life of every human being.

I NEED YOU

I need you
You need me
We need each other
Oh, how much I need you
Oh, how dear you are to me
Oh, how much I miss you
Just because I need you
I need you for my heart to be complete
I need you for my joy to be full
I need you for my eyes to be two
I need you for peace to reign in me
Oh how I need you
Just show me that you need me
By loving me
For that is the only way
To appreciate me for needing you

I CAN'T SAY NO

At a point in my life
I found myself withering
Just like the flowers of the field
Just because I was in search
Of my missing limb
All hope seems lost
But hope is the only light
That shines in the stormy path
It kept shining for me
With perseverance as my companion
With love as my path
I moved to the point where
I can't say no
This showed me my limb
Waiting patiently and adoringly for me
Oh, how pretty was my limb
That I can't say no

THIS THING CALLED LOVE

O this thing word
O this thing
How I wish you know it!
This thing called love
The greatest magnet
The greatest charms
What it has done to man
Remains uncountable
Because of this thing called love
Two different people
From different places
From different families
Are attracted and magnetized
Strongly drawn to each other
All in the name of love
It does not count on barriers
For its above barriers
Religion cannot be compared
On the same scale with love
Physical appearance too cannot be compared with love

Oh, this thing called love
It has made men
Look stupid when they are not
It has made some look foolish
When they are actually wise
It has made some seem irrational
When they are rational
It is the only language
That can be heard by all races
It is the bridge

That unites two banks.
To understand the language
Of this thing called love
Is the beginning of life...
It was this thing called love
That changed the history of humanity
For the first man who spoke of it loudly
Changed history from BC to AD
Thus, Christ became
The first man to look foolish
Dying for those who are not of his family,
Nor from His race,
It has the most significant power in it
This force pushed Martin Luther King, Jr.
To take the risk of his life
Mahatma Gandhi spoke the same language of love
And India got her freedom
Nelson Mandela and Steve Biko
Spoke the same in South Africa
And freedom was the end result
When after an extended period of apartheid
Which many paid with their blood
This is the price of love

The most exceptional people in the history of humanity
Are those who died for the sake of love
Those who moved the world positively
Are those people
Who in their lifetime
In season and out of season
Have always aspired to do one thing: love.

This is the thing which every other person may not do

When things are not moving well.
Love is their deeds not words.
It is love that has made them great
If they end up dying, it is
for this thing called: love.
Christ is the definition of love and the reason for
This thing called love.

IT SEEMS TO BE BLIND

It seems to be blind
Because of the way we see it
Because we lack understanding.
Of course, the blind do not see
But it does not mean they don't feel
Even though they see not
They still reserve other senses.
So, to say that love is blind
Is for me a lack of understanding
Love does not deal on appearances
Love does not deal on instinct
Love has reason
That's why
It seems to be blind
It looks on values
Instead of artificialities
It focuses on originality
Instead of trivialities
It appreciates nature
More than any other thing
This is why
It seems to be blind
The magnetic force of love
Has the natural tendency
Of overcoming what artificial eye values
This is why it looks bizarre
When love exists between two people
Who for people are incompatible
Yet for love
They are best of all

Have you fallen in love?
It melts humans like vapor
It makes humans moderate
It makes hardened hearts soft
It brings down the mighty
From their thrones
So strong the force of love
That king can give up his throne
So strong the force of love
That a king can give up his life
So strong the power of love
That one can offer his or her life
For the other
So, dominating this force of love
That even the devil fears to love
When there is love
Peace and tranquility
Merge together to form a unity
It can lead one to do the things
Which no other power
Can push one to do
The bible says God is love
And love is God
That is why when you are
Under the spell of love
You have only one focus
Everything around seems to be nothing
And that is why
It seems to be blind

HOW CAN THERE BE LIFE?

How can there be life?
Without love
How can there be life?
Without hope
How can there be life?
Without people
How can there be joy?
Without sharing
How can one be lonely?
When there are people like you
To garnish people's loneliness
To encourage the despairing
To give joy to the sorrowful
There can never be life
When good people like you
Are out of place
With your absence in people's life
Life becomes misery
And a life of misery
Is as good as death
For life is meant to be enjoyed
Remove joy from life
Everything becomes sour
In that situation
How can there be life?
When there is no joy
When everything is meaningless
How can there be life?
Without love

How can there be
Life without love?
Then life ceases to have meaning
To live a life without love
Is to be a jobless being
To live a life without love
Is like a beautiful car without an engine
To live a life without love
Is like a man who is without life
To live a life without love
Is like sorrow without consolation
To live a life without love
Is like Peter without the rock
To live life without love
Is like an alien in a foreign land
Our life is centered on love
We live in love
For our breath and life is centered on love
Everything we have
Is a gift from love
They came to us out of love
And we are expected to give back in love
Then to live life without love
Is grievous harm to ourselves
Hampering and hindering our growth
Closing the windows of our blessing
Because there cannot be dividends
Of good things
Which come from God and man
When we are living
Life without love

WASTING TIME

We waste our time
If we are living without loving
Since living without loving
Is like laboring without earning
Who will prefer to be working,
Without the fruits of earning?
No one in a good state of mind
Will like to spend their time
On what will add no value to their lives
So of what value is our life when we do not love?

When love is the only thing that will make life fruitful
Then why waste the time not loving?
If we gain nothing not loving
Then why waste the time not loving?
The only time we have used well on earth
Is the time we spent loving
The only time we have spent living
Is the time we spent loving
Therefore, let us start loving today
By wasting no more time
For a life without love
Is wasting time

THE TWO-WAY ROUTE

The two-way route
Is to love
And to be loved.
You loved first
Accept to be loved
To reject God's love
Is the damnation of one.
Peter rejected it
The master's caution
Pushed him to accept it.
For thus he asserted
Consume me with your love
By washing me through and through.
Judas rejected to be loved,
Despite the warning of the master
He preferred to die
Rather than plead for mercy

The two-way route
Is loving one another
And allowing God to love us
This is the way of life
To live one-sided of it
Is an incomplete life
So, my friend,
I say love and be loved
For if you cannot love
You cannot be loved
Alas! For the measure you use on others
Will be the same measure to be used on you.

THE CAPTAIN IS THE SERVANT

O how it sounds
So bizarre to the ear
That the captain is the servant
Very ridiculous to be thought of
Yet, the captain is the servant
At the forefront he is,
Setting the ship on the sail
Towards North, South, East, and West
For he is the leader
They claim he is not the servant,
Yet, he is the servant
Uneasy lies the head
That wears the crown
Since he agreed to sail the ship
He should accept the lot
Of being the servant
Because he does the work of servant
Taking others and their properties
To their various destinations
Confirming the stewardship

To be a captain, therefore,
You must possess the humility
And obedience of a servant
For every captain ought to be a servant
If you don't open the door of love
That exists in your heart
The entry to service remains closed
But open the door of love
The entrance to service opens
A good captain therefore
Is a good servant
Who has the doors of love and service open?

EUCHARISTIC HEART

What does it mean?
To say that one has Eucharistic heart
It doesn't mean one who receives the Eucharist
Nor does it depict only the Christians
No! For that is far from the point
Eucharistic heart:
Is a heart that is E- Empathetic
Is a heart that is U- Understanding
Is a heart that is C- Charitable
Is a heart that is H- Humane
Is a heart that is A- Affectionate
Is a heart that is R- Respectful
Is a heart that is I- Intimate
Is a heart that is S- Selfless
Is a heart that is T- Truthful
All these are found in a Eucharistic heart
Any heart can be Eucharistic
If you add that it is a heart that is in love
Is a heart that is caring
Check the heart and know
Whether all or any of these are missing
Work hard to gain them or it
So that your heart will be
A place of peace and joy,
Where millions will run for solace,
And get the consolation
Which is due to the hearts
That are eager to share
That peace and joy
Which are lost in all the hearts
That are not Eucharistic.

TO BE A MAN IS TO EXPRESS LOVE

Do you really know what it means to be a man?
Do you think that being a man is being pugnacious?
Or to destroy and maltreat others?
No! That is not the meaning of being a man
Man often is regarded as the strongest of beings
Thus, the cause of the axiom "Be a man!"
Being a man means loving
Being able to show love
For that is the most significant energy consumer
It cannot be explained by all
Hence the scripture says
We who are strong
Ought to bear the failings of the weak
To do this is what it means to be a man
To be a man is to express love
Which can only be shown
By those who are strong of heart.

NEVER WILL I SEPARATE FROM YOU AGAIN

O my love
O my soul
O my breath
How wonderful thou art
For a thousand times
I sought for you
Day and night with hope
With a million moments of faith and hope
Because I know I must find you
But there thou art waiting for me
To unite the missing heart
So that our hearts may be one
I have seen you my love, my soul, and my breath
Never will I separate from you again
O Lord my God

CHARITY IS...

Charity is love done out of Care and Concern
Charity is joy when done out of Humaneness and Holiness
Charity is sacrifice when done out of Altruism and
Affection
Charity is freedom when done out of Respect and
Responsibility
Charity is hope when done out of Integrity and Interest
Charity is faith when done out of Trust and Truthfulness
Charity is obedience when done out of Yearning and Yes

CHARITY BRINGS LOVE

Charity brings love
Love brings peace
Peace brings joy
Joy brings hope
Hope brings faith
Faith brings trust
Trust brings truth
If charity is a sacrifice
The sacrifice from myself
Of my things
In my own time
For the sake of love.

I MUST LOVE LIKE YOU

In You, I see my love
In You, I see my peace
In You, I see my hope
Your love is so great
That for me to be happy
I must love like You

JUST BECAUSE OF LOVE

Many will pay millions
Others will offer their lives
Thousands will give all they have
Billions will desire greatly
Just to be your friend
But I offered nothing
Yet what others could not get
Even when they had offered everything
Was given to me freely
Just because of love
I promise forever my sincerest love

THAT I HAVE SOMEBODY LIKE YOU

The whole world envies me
Not because I am fine
Not because I am rich
Nor is it because I can speak well
Nor sing well
Just because of one thing:
That I have somebody like You!
This is what they have all desired to have
But failed all the time
I will forever bask in the presence of love-
Because I have somebody like You!

BUT FOR THE SAKE OF LOVE

Many climbed the mountain
Some on the treetops
Some on the housetops
Some on top of others
Just to have a glimpse
Of thy beauty
Some failed to break their necks
Some their legs
But for the sake of love
I stood on the ground
And saw thy beauty
Thank you for accepting my imperfect love
I'll remain steadfast in love,
with your help and grace.

WHAT IS NEW ABOUT THIS LOVE?

What is new about this love?
Which God created
The prophets prophesied it
The ancient fathers spoke of it
Yet, it was never old
Something is new about this love
Christ made it fresh and new
When He taught us
Selflessness by giving his life
Sacrificed for us all
The apostles embraced it
And sacrificed everything for it, even their lives
Martin Luther King junior spoke of it to the crowds
Gandhi lived out this love
And died to liberate his brethren
Anyone who encounters this love
Will become new

O GREAT LOVE

Anyone who rejects you is gone
Thousands of years ago
The first world of men was destroyed
Just because they rejected you
A new world of men was formed
For them to accept you
But when they rejected you
Forty days became forty years
Serpents devoured some of them
Only they that accepted you remained
The prophets of old were murdered
Just because they spoke of you
And because men rejected you.

In human history
The cause of all violence is out of rejection
And denial of you
Any society formed without reverence for you
Is destined to ruin
Throughout human history
All attempts of humans from every era and place
Have tried to dethrone you
But thou art invincible.

The modern world has made effort
To dethrone you
By enthroning materialism, technology
Selfishness, individualism, and capitalism
And all sorts of crimes -
Justified by all sorts of mentally ill thinking.
Though many say they desire you,

Yet, only a few would die for you.
Many will instead trample your ways, murder you
Then give everything for you
And this world will never
ever know peace
Unless they enthrone you
O, Great Love!

FOR LOVE KNOWS NO BOUNDARY

The daylight comes and fades away
The rain falls and dries up
Rivers overflow their banks in spring
Oceans overflow their boundaries
All these things happen mostly during the raining season
But with the winter season
These maintain their boundaries
But my love for you
Will be in season and out of season
It will be eternal
For love knows no limitation.

WHEN I THINK OF YOU

When I think of you
Joy fills my soul
When I think of you
I feel the completeness of my being
When I think of you
I feel your presence
When I think of you
I do the most significant things in life
When I think of you
I bless the day I met you
When I think of you
Everything else becomes useless
When I think of you
I become like a child in the mother's womb
When I think of you
You fill the joy of my life
When I think of you
I feel like being in your presence forever
When I think of you
My burdens are made light
When I think of you
I wish to be yours and yours alone
When I think of you
I conquer all my temptations
Because you O God are my love
Because you O God are my strength
I will forever think of you
When I do this, this is the success in life.

JUST BECAUSE YOU LOVE ME

You say "go on"
When despair blocks my way
You say, "stand firm."
When fear locks me in
You say, "be patient."
When time seems to run out on me
You say, "be hopeful."
When the journey seems to be tasking
You say "listen."
When I seem to wander away
You say, "I am here."
When I seem to be alone
You say, "come sit with me."
When I feel my sin is unforgivable
You say, "I love you."
When I think no one loves me
You say, "your love is here."
When I have done things well on this earth
You say, "I will be with you forever."
Just because you love me.

WAIT FOR ME MY LOVE

Wait for me
Hold hands with me in love
And move on the slippery path
To hold me when I am about to fall
For this journey is hard
If I walk alone on this path
Filled with enemies
But with you by my side
I shall not walk alone
With you by my side
I shall not fall
With you by my side
The journey will be smooth
With you on my side
All is well with me
I love you dear Lord
Wait for me, my love

GIVE ME

Give me eyes
That I may see the beauty of your love
Give me a nose
That I may breathe the spirit of your love
Give me ears
That I may hear of thy love
Give me a mouth
That I may speak of your love
Give me hands
That I may work for your love
Give me legs
That I may walk in the path of your love
Give me a heart
Where I may carry your passion
Give me brain
That I may think of your greatness
For when you give these to me
I can share them with others in turn.

JUST BECAUSE OF LOVE

I can do anything
Just because of your love
I can sacrifice the most precious gift
Just because of your love
I can go any mile
Just because of your love
I am ready for any pain
Just because of your love
For there's no greater love
Than to give one's life
For the sake of love.

I HOPE TO SEE YOU AGAIN

Say goodbye O friend!
Say farewell O dearest!
Promise to see me again O my love
Say not: "it's over," O good one
For though I miss you now
I hope to see you again
Though we part now
One day, we shall meet to part no more
In that land where
Our lives continue in love
The bond that kept us together
While we lived

THE PASSION OF LOVE

I was called a fool
I lost all my friends
And all my possessions
Even my life lost all meaning
Because of the fire
Which comes from you
The passion of love
So strong as the power
Of death, life, and celebration
Amidst these three powers
Each happens on a desire
Towards love for any of them.

PRAYER FOR REAL LOVE

Lord Jesus Christ,
We are your brothers and sisters,
For your love,
You gave your life for our sake,
Though we were sinners,
Let this kind of love grow within us,
So that we will always be ready,
To show this kind of love to all
Do not allow the snares of the evil one
To hamper or destroy this love.
We have searched for love,
Until we found it,
God is love and love is God.
Let this love reign in us
So that forever we may remain
In this love and die in it,
Loving each other
Blessed by you
I found real love
Through Christ our Lord. Amen, I love you!

EVERYWHERE LOVE

Everywhere love
In the highest heaven love
In the deepest depth love
In the islands love
In the oceans love
In the forests love
In the lands love
Among humans: love
Among animals: love
Among plants: love
Everywhere: love
Everyday: love
Love! Love!! Love!!!
Everywhere love
All the time love
With the eye, you see love
With the ear, you hear love
With the mouth, you speak love
With the head, you think love
With the heart, you feel love
We are healed with love
Everywhere love

EVERYTHING NEEDS LOVE

Everybody needs love
Everything needs love
You can feel the power of love
Even in the far distant isles love
When you are loved by someone
You will always feel the love
When someone you love thinks of you
No matter the distance
You feel the impact of that love
Love heals hypertension
Love heals hatred
Love brings progress
Love brings unity
When you feel loved
What is the result? Happiness
When you feel loved
You feel needed
When you feel loved
It brings out the best in you
It pays to love
Everything changes with the power of love.

DON'T CONFUSE LUST WITH LOVE

Don't confuse lust with love
Love leads to happiness
Thus, defined as
Live and Overcome Vices Everywhere
When you love, you live
When you love, you overcome
When you love, you are virtuous
When you love, you are everywhere.
But when you lust
You are in sorrow
You lose Understanding and Suffer Tragedy
This happens when the evil one is at work
Therefore, I say to you
When you lust, you lose
When you lust, you lack understanding
When you lust, you suffer
When you lust, you end up in tragedy

So, give love
To the North - give love
To the South - give love
To the East - give love
To the West - give love
Everywhere needs love
Everything needs love
Therefore, give love
You need love
I need love
Everyone needs love.

WHAT CAN YOU DO FOR LOVE?

Many people have done many things
Just because of love
Christ gave his life
For the sake of love
This changed history from BC to AD
Great men in history
Are immortalized for ages
For nothing, but love
Heroes who are celebrated
Are those who died for love
The sands of time are changed
By the power of love
Those who died for love
Can never be forgotten
Because love is eternal
Do you want to be eternal?
Do you want to be great?
Do you want to be remembered?
Do you want to be a hero?
What can you do for love?

ONLY LOVE

What has gone around the world?
What brings joy to humanity?
What can conquer any obstacle?
What can turn even the darkest things around?
Only love
Only love can change anything
Only love can bring novelty
Only love can reign

I WILL BE GLAD

When you love me
I will be glad
When I love you
I will be glad
When love is my friend
I will be glad
When love envelopes me
I will be glad
When love shines on me
I will be glad
Indeed I will be glad
When I live the life of love
I will be glad when I share my love
I will be glad
When people need my love
I will be glad
If I suffer for the sake of love
I will be glad
When people hate me because of love
I will be glad
When my life feels the presence of love
I will be glad
I don't know where my path is leading
But I will be glad
If I end up being loved
If I end up loving God
If God's love is with me
If I end up loving others
I will be glad,
I will be glad,
I will be glad.

IT CAN KEEP US TOGETHER

It can keep us together
And bring us together
When we share it together
Since it brings all together
For when we share it together
We will always live better
Because it makes life better
When we share love together
Or hope and faith together
We may forever be together
Because love, faith and hope will keep us together
Families will remain together
If they share these together
Nations will be together
When families are together
Because when we see things together
And share it together
Then we will always remain together.
If we do not share love, faith and hope together
Nothing can keep us together
Nothing even wealth can keep us together
If wealth can keep us together
The whole world would have been together
We are divided because we are not together
The love that'll keep us together
Has lost the faith that'll keep us together
Hardly is there any hope that we'll be together
But if we share love together
It can keep us together.

TEN GREATEST THINGS THAT CAN BE SAID
ABOUT LOVE

God is love.
Love is a mystery.
Love cannot be explained.
Love works beyond human imagination.
Love fills the whole world.
Love has power.
Love is the most significant force in the universe.
Love is life.
Love is a network that connects everything.
Love is a reality.

TWENTY THINGS THAT CAN PRODUCE LOVE

1. Encountering others in love.
2. Going out to love others first.
3. Thinking about God and others first.
4. Doing everything for the sake of love.
5. Imitating Christ, the author of love.
6. Make yourself an object of love.
7. A desire to love and be loved.
8. Never give room for any suspicion.
9. Never listen to gossip.
10. Forgive those who wronged you.
11. Be ready to sacrifice always.
12. Do not be selective in loving.
13. Uproot hatred wherever it germinates.
14. Pray always for love.
15. Think of God who is love and source of love.
16. Open up to the person you love.
17. Avoid fear and despair in trying to love.
18. Never force someone to love you or allow another to force you into loving them - for love is a free gift.
19. Know what you want and go for it.
20. Differentiate between love and lust.

FIFTY THINGS THAT CAN BE SAID ABOUT LOVE

1. Love bears all things.
2. Love knows all things.
3. The world is nothing without love.
4. Love is powerful.
5. Love attracts.
6. Love unites.
7. We get the best out of love.
8. When we are loved, we are happy.
9. With love, you can do all things.
10. Love is the hope of the despairing.
11. Love is the strength of the weak.
12. Love is the health of the sick.
13. Love is the light of those in darkness.
14. In love, we see our real selves.
15. Love understands all things.
16. Love creates new things.
17. We are indebted to love everybody.
18. Love knows no boundary.
19. Love works on openness.
20. Love breeds success.
21. Love is an ocean of life.
22. Love is the key to heaven.
23. In love, we were all made.
24. We are expected to live in love.
25. Love conquers everywhere.
26. Love turns sinners to saints.
27. Love turns hopeless people into hopeful people.
28. Love kills hatred.
29. Love is radical.
30. God is love.
31. Love is great.

32. Without love we are finished.
33. Love never gives up.
34. Love sees from a higher point of view.
35. Love looks before it reaps.
36. Love has eyes.
37. Love is not blind but deals on choice.
38. Love works as a network.
39. Love is a feeling.
40. Love can be felt by the willing ones.
41. Love is a deed and not only words.
42. Without love, there can be no family.
43. Without love, there can be no marriage.
44. Love is the success of every marriage.
45. Love is the strength of every friendship.
46. Love is pure.
47. Love is different from lust.
48. Love sharpens the intellect.
49. Love is the key to every heart.
50. Love is a free gift.

CONCLUSION

There are many things to be said about love. We have to define love according to our own makeup without removing the original content of love. Love must involve freedom and trust in those who are involved. Love must point towards God who is the source of love, and love must be for the common good. Love must transcend ethnic and cultural diversities. It must be felt everywhere just as we feel the love of God everywhere in every day.

If we must love, we must be ready to sacrifice our time, energy, our comfort, and whatever we have for the sake of those we love. If God can sacrifice the only beloved Son to teach us the meaning of love, then what is most important to us can as well go the way of sacrifice for the sake of love. In love, we have to give without counting the cost of anything about our life. In life, all we think when we love is the good of the person we love more than our own good.

Made in the USA
Middletown, DE
15 June 2021